YOUR GUIDE to LIFE on EARTH

Gill Arbuthnott

ILLUSTRATED BY Marc Mones

Crabtree Publishing Company
www.crabtreebooks.com

Crabtree Publishing Company
www.crabtreebooks.com
1-800-387-7650

Published in Canada
Crabtree Publishing
616 Welland Avenue
St. Catharines, ON
L2M 5V6

Published in the United States
Crabtree Publishing
PMB 59051
350 Fifth Ave, 59th Floor
New York, NY 10118

Published by Crabtree Publishing Company in 2016

For all my Biology pupils —
I told you life was amazing!

Author: Gill Arbuthnott

Project coordinator: Kathy Middleton

Editor: Wendy Scavuzzo

Proofreader: Janine Deschenes

Prepress technician: Tammy McGarr

Print and production coordinator:
  Margaret Amy Salter

Science Consultant: Shirley Duke

First published in 2015 by A & C Black, an imprint of Bloomsbury Publishing Plc
Copyright © 2015 A & C Black

Text copyright © 2015 Gill Arbuthnott
Illustration copyright © 2015 Marc Mones

Additional images © Shutterstock

Printed in Canada/022016/MA20151130

Library and Archives Canada Cataloguing in Publication

Arbuthnott, Gill, author
    Your guide to life on Earth / Gill Arbuthnott ; Marc Mones, illustrator.

(Drawn to science, illustrated guides to key science concepts)
Includes index.
ISBN 978-0-7787-2243-4 (bound).--ISBN 978-0-7787-2251-9 (paperback)

    1. Life (Biology)--Juvenile literature. I. Mones, Marc, illustrator
II. Title.

QH501.A73 2016   j570   C2015-907107-0

Library of Congress Cataloging-in-Publication Data

Names: Arbuthnott, Gill, author. | Mones, Marc, illustrator.
Title: Your guide to life on Earth / Gill Arbuthnott ; illustrated by Marc Mones.
Description:Crabtree Publishing Company, 2016. | Series: Drawn to science : illustrated guides to key science concepts | Includes index.
Identifiers: LCCN 2015042099| ISBN 9780778722434 (reinforced library binding : alk. paper) | ISBN 9780778722519 (pbk. : alk. paper)
Subjects: LCSH: Life (Biology)--Juvenile literature. | Biology--Classification--Juvenile literature.
Classification: LCC QH309.2 .A73 2016 | DDC 570--dc23
LC record available at http://lccn.loc.gov/2015042099

Contents

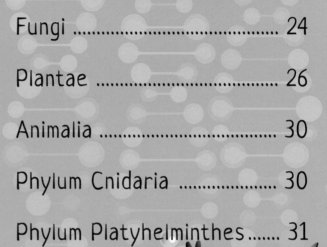

Introduction

If you're reading this book, then you're a living organism. And assuming that you're on planet Earth, then you're a human. You are also surrounded by countless other types of living things. About 1.4 million species have been named so far, but there may be tens of millions more waiting to be discovered.

What exactly is life? What is a living thing? What makes a real flower different from an artificial one? If trees and tables are both made of wood, does that mean they're both alive? And what about a wooly sweater, that used to be part of a sheep…

Confused? Don't worry. *Your Guide to Life on Earth* will help you understand what life is, and take you on a tour of some of the most extraordinary examples of life on Earth.

So, how did life begin?

Turn the page to discover some possible answers…

How Life Began

Planet Earth is around 4,500 million years old. As far as we know, life on Earth began about 3,500 million years ago. This is just an estimate since there was no one around to see it. Scientists have figured out a number of possible ways life on Earth could have happened. The theory below is one of the best known.

Primordial soup

Millions of years ago, Earth was very different from the planet we live on now. It's believed that the atmosphere, which is the makeup of gases surrounding Earth, was composed of the gases methane, ammonia, hydrogen, and water vapor; instead of the mixture of oxygen, nitrogen, and carbon dioxide we breathe today. There were no animals or plants, no **bacteria**, no cells, no forms of life at all. There was just a "soup" of simple chemicals in the oceans. This is sometimes called **primordial** soup. Primordial means the very first, or earliest.

Life from lightning?

Earth was a very violent planet back then, with volcanic eruptions and huge electrical storms. Bolts of lightning frequently struck the oceans, and high levels of ultraviolet (**UV**) light from the sun bombarded the water with **radiation**. This provided energy which allowed the simple chemicals to join together to make more complicated chemicals. Scientists have carried out experiments that attempt to recreate this, and have found that **amino acids**—the building blocks from which **proteins** are made—will form under these conditions.

Eventually, **molecules** were formed that had the ability to copy themselves. These molecules were related to the **DNA** found in the cells of all living things today. And so, life began.

Not on Earth!

There are some theories that suggest that life didn't begin on Earth at all! Some scientists think that the molecules on which life is based may have arrived from another planet on a **meteorite** or a comet.

Researchers have found evidence of these molecules on one of Jupiter's moons and on **asteroids**. We may never know exactly how life on Earth began, but we now know exactly how to decide if something is a living organism or not. Turn the page to find out more.

Jupiter

Meet Mrs. Gren

So, what is life? There are some quite complicated explanations of the characteristics of life, which are the processes that every single living thing carries out. But we'll keep it simple. Our guide will be Mrs. Gren. Who exactly is Mrs. Gren? She's just a handy way of remembering the first letters of the seven basic characteristics of life!

Movement
Reproduction
Sensitivity
Growth
Respiration
Excretion
Nutrition

Movement

This can mean a number of things: movement within a single cell, movement of parts of an animal or plant, or **locomotion**, which is the ability to move from place to place. There's a tiny transport system inside every cell which moves materials to where they are needed. Even animals that spend all their lives in one place can move parts of their bodies.

For instance, sea anemones are stuck to rocks in the sea but can move their tentacles. Most animals move from place to place, and they use lots of different methods to do so: swimming, crawling, walking, running, jumping, swinging, and flying.

But even if things move around inside their cells, plants don't move—or do they? They don't usually move from place to place, but they do move. It's just that they do it so slowly that it's hard for us to notice.

There are exceptions, though. The Venus flytrap has special pairs of leaves that close very fast when an insect walks over them, and the sensitive plant closes its delicate leaves in the rain or when touched.

Reproduction

Reproduction is the process of producing **offspring**, or new organisms. This is how a species survives through generations. Very simple organisms such as bacteria just split in two. In some plants, a piece can break off and grow into a whole new plant. This is called **asexual reproduction**. However, most plants and animals use **sexual reproduction**. This is when a cell from the male parent joins with a cell from the female parent.

Sensitivity

We don't mean bursting into tears! Sensitivity is the ability to respond to changes in the environment or inside the organism itself. Plant shoots grow toward light, and their roots grow into the ground due to gravity. Animals use their senses to detect food and predators. You respond to changes in temperature by shivering or sweating. Organisms also respond to changes inside their own bodies. For instance, your brain is constantly altering your heartbeat and breathing rate to keep conditions perfect for your cells.

C-c-can s-s-someone get me a s-s-sweater!

Growth

Huge oak trees begin as small acorns. Humans start as a single cell the size of a period. Kangaroos are born about the size of a jelly bean—everything grows. Animals get to a certain size and stop growing, but many plants continue to grow throughout their lives. Growth is an **irreversible** increase in size or mass. If you drink 17 fluid ounces (500 ml) of water, you will gain 17 ounces (500 g) in mass. But you haven't grown because the change is reversible. You will lose the water either through sweat or urination (pee).

I wonder if I will grow to be that big.

Respiration

Have you ever wondered why you need to eat? Eating is how your body gets the raw materials it needs for growth and repair. But food is also the fuel you use to give your body energy to do everything. **Respiration** is the process by which cells break down chemicals such as glucose (sugar made by food) to release the energy they contain. It's a bit like burning oil or wood to release energy as heat and light, but of course there aren't tiny fires burning in your cells! Instead, the energy is released in a much slower and more controlled way.

Excretion

A lot of chemical reactions take place in every living cell. Some of these reactions create substances that aren't needed or might be **toxic** to the organism. **Excretion** is the process by which waste products are removed from the organism. For example, most cells produce carbon dioxide gas when they respire. Humans and animals excrete this gas every time they breathe out. Water is another waste product produced by chemical reactions inside humans and animals. The waste water is removed by being excreted through urine.

Nutrition

As far as animals are concerned, **nutrition** refers to eating, whether it's a crisp, juicy apple for you, a meal of blood for a flea, or some delicious rotting meat for a maggot! Plants make their own food by a process called **photosynthesis**. Using a special molecule called **chlorophyll**, which is what gives them their green color, they can use the energy in sunlight to convert carbon dioxide gas and water into sugar. Imagine if humans could do that… we would get fat in summer when it was sunny, and thin in winter when it was gloomy. And we would be green, of course!

Cells

All living things are made of cells, but what exactly is a cell? No one knew they existed until the 1600s. Scientist Robert Hooke invented a microscope that could magnify things so they looked 50 times larger than they actually were. He looked at a very thin slice of cork and saw it was made of tiny walled spaces. These reminded him of the cells in which monks lived, and so the name "cell" stuck.

There are two basic types of cells. **Prokaryotic cells** are very simple, and are only found in bacteria. **Eukaryotic cells** are much more complex, and make up everything from the single-celled fungus yeast, to humans.

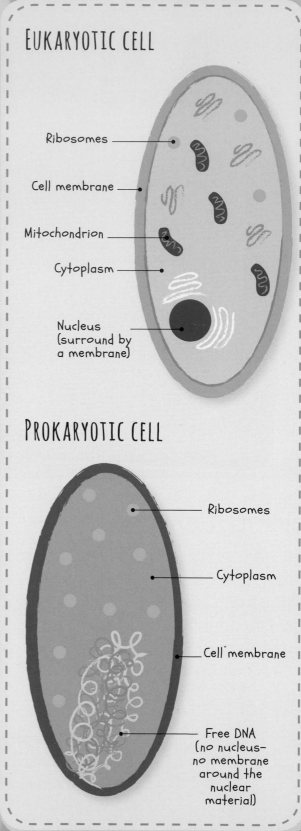

EUKARYOTIC CELL

Ribosomes

Cell membrane

Mitochondrion

Cytoplasm

Nucleus (surround by a membrane)

PROKARYOTIC CELL

Ribosomes

Cytoplasm

Cell membrane

Free DNA (no nucleus— no membrane around the nuclear material)

Robert Hooke

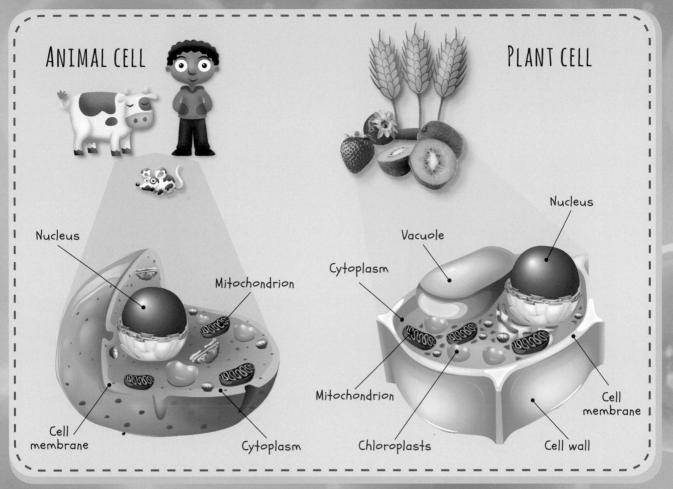

ANIMAL CELL

PLANT CELL

Nucleus

Mitochondrion

Cell membrane

Cytoplasm

Nucleus

Vacuole

Cytoplasm

Mitochondrion

Chloroplasts

Cell wall

Cell membrane

Cell jobs

Plant and animal cells are different from each other, and they have different jobs to do. For example, animals have nerve cells that may be more than 3 feet (1 m) long, red blood cells that have no **nucleus**, brain cells that each communicate with 10,000 other cells, and white blood cells that crawl through their bodies searching for bacteria. Plant cells are adapted to make food, take in water, sting, support the plant, and transport substances up and down the stem.

And I thought cells were just tiny blobs!

Single-celled organisms

Many living things manage to carry out all the Mrs. Gren characteristics in one single cell. Some of these organisms are like tiny animals, and others are like very tiny plants. However, not all of them are easy to categorize. For instance, there is one type of organism that has chlorophyll, like a plant, and a simple eye, like an animal.

Sponge soup? Do I eat it or have a bath in it?

Multicellular organisms

Most organisms, including humans, are made up of many millions of cells working together. In these **multicellular** organisms, there are many of different types of cells, each with a special job to do. Some of the simplest multicellular organisms are sponges. They only have a few types of cells. They don't need to be more complex because all they do is sit on a rock, let water flow through them, and filter out tiny particles of food. Amazingly, if you break apart a sponge into small pieces, and leave it for a while, the individual cells will join together again to re-form the sponge!

Natural sponges

Slime molds

Slime molds are even stranger than sponges. They live most of their lives as single cells, but if their food runs out, they release chemicals that let them find other slime mold cells. These cells join together to form a multicellular phase called a slug (not like the ones in your garden, though). The slug slithers along until it comes to open ground, then the cells climb on top of each other to form something like a tiny mushroom.

Some of the cells then turn into **spores** and float away. This is how the slime mold reproduces. The cells that formed the "stalk" of the mushroom die.

Scientists have found that slime molds can solve mazes! Remember, this is an organism without a head or a brain!

Slime molds join together to make something like a tiny mushroom.

15

Organizing Organisms

If aliens arrived on Earth and took samples of every living thing, they would have a very big heap of organisms to sort out—and they'd need a very big spaceship! They would sort the organisms by looking at similarities and differences, and gradually put them all into groups. Scientists on Earth have already done this for all the species they know about. This process is called **classification**.

Classification

The first attempts to sort organisms separated everything into two piles, or Kingdoms: Plants and Animals. However, as scientists learned more about the organisms they were studying, they realized that not everything fit into these groups.

The system most commonly used now has six Kingdoms: Plants, Animals, Protists, Fungi, Archaebacteria, Eubacteria. These six Kingdoms are the most basic divisions. By comparing the features of different organisms within the same Kingdom, scientists can divide each Kingdom into smaller and smaller groups, each with more features in common. The smallest groups are called Species. The next page shows how each group is divided down into a smaller category.

Each Kingdom is divided into → Phyla

Each Phylum is divided into → Classes

Each Class is divided into → Orders

Each Order is divided into → Families

Each Family is divided into → Genera

Each Genus is divided into → Species

The classification system looks like tree roots. Each level branches out into groups, and each group branches out into more groups.

This is an example of the groups, from largest to smallest, showing how humans are classified.

LARGEST GROUP

The organisms in this group have just a few basic features in common. It contains every type of animal.

SMALLEST GROUP

Every organism of the same species has many features in common. All the animals in the species **Homo sapiens** are humans.

Groups	Human Classification
Kingdom	Animals
Phylum	Chordates
Class	Mammals
Order	Primates
Family	Hominids
Genus	*Homo*
Species	*sapiens*

Naming Organisms

For centuries, people gave local names to plants and animals. This was very confusing since it meant the same plant could end up with many different names. For instance, foxgloves were also called dead man's bells, fairy thimbles, and witch's gloves. It became very difficult for scientists from different areas to be sure they were all talking about the same plant. Someone needed to sort things out! Enter Carl Linnaeus.

Carl Linnaeus

Linnaeus takes charge

Linnaeus was a Swedish botanist who decided that a new naming system was badly needed. He turned to **Latin** for help. During the 18th century, Latin was the language of learning. If you went to any university in any European country, you had to know Latin. Linnaeus came up with a system in which every living thing would have a two-part Latin name that would be agreed on and used by scientists everywhere.

Linnaeus's system

In Linneaus's system, the foxglove is called *Digitalis purpurea* and humans are *Homo sapiens*. The first part of the name is the genus (a bit like the surname) and the second part is the species (a bit like a first name). Very closely related organisms share their genus name. *Homo neanderthalensis* is Neanderthal man, the nearest relative to modern humans, and there are over 20 *Digitalis* species.

More than just names...

The other interesting thing about these names is that most of them describe something about the organism. For *Digitalis purpurea*, or foxglove, *Digitalis* means "finger-like," and the flowers of a foxglove fit perfectly onto your fingers. *Purpurea* means "purple," the most common color of the foxglove. In *Homo sapiens*, *Homo* means "man" and *sapiens* means "wise." *Neanderthalensis* refers to where the first fossils were found— the Neander valley in Germany.

Now that we've looked at the basics, let's start our tour of life on Earth!

The Six Kingdoms

The Six Kingdoms are the biggest of the groups into which all living organisms are classified. The organisms in each Kingdom share some basic features. But there's one group that doesn't fit into any of the Kingdoms: **viruses**.

> Wow! That virus looks like a spacecraft!

Bacteriophage

Viruses

This is a group that made scientists who were classifying organisms scratch their heads. A virus isn't a cell—it's just a bit of DNA wrapped up in protein. Everything else that has DNA is a living thing, but they are also made of cells. However, new viruses can be created. Isn't that reproduction?

Actually, viruses can only get themselves reproduced if they take over a living cell to do it for them. They are not living things. They seem to have some of the Mrs. Gren characteristics, but a living organism must have all the characteristics, and must be made of cells.

Diseases

All viruses cause diseases because they destroy cells when they use them to make new viruses. Some are mild diseases, such as the common cold. But others, such as **smallpox** and HIV (Human Immunodeficiency Virus, which causes **AIDS**), are deadly.

However, they're not all bad. There is a group of viruses called **bacteriophages** which only target bacteria. Some bacteria cause diseases, so perhaps we can use these viruses to kill them and prevent those diseases.

Protista

The Protist Kingdom is a very mixed group. It's like that cupboard where you put things that don't quite belong anywhere else. Living things that aren't animals, plants, fungi, or bacteria end up in this Kingdom.

A lot of protists are single-celled organisms found in water. If you collect water from a pond and look at it under a microscope—or even a good magnifying glass—you'll see a lot of them.

Amoeba proteus, under a microscope

Malaria

Some protists cause diseases. **Malaria** is caused by a protist called *Plasmodium*, which is carried and spread by some types of mosquitoes. When they bite, they inject the *Plasmodium* into their victim's blood. Malaria affects about two million people every year and kills around 500,000.

Eubacteria and Archaebacteria

The Bacteria Kingdom includes two Kingdoms: Archaebacteria, which are bacteria that live in extreme conditions such as hotsprings; and Eubacteria, which are all the other types of bacteria. You're probably thinking "Yuck! Germs!" But most bacteria are harmless, and some are actually very helpful.

Each bacterium is a single prokaryotic cell. They are the simplest forms of life and they exist almost everywhere, including all over you! Your skin is covered in them, no matter how clean you are, and your stomach is full of them, too.

In fact, you have more bacteria cells than human cells! The bacteria in your digestive system help you process food. If they all got destroyed, it could make you feel quite sick. The bacteria on your skin don't do any harm, although some of them could if they get into a wound.

Here are a few stars of the bacteria world:

◎ *Lactobacillus*: Very useful to humans who like cheese and yogurt, because this bacterium changes milk into those products.

◎ *Geobacter*: Can gobble up pollutants from oil spills. Even better, it may be able to generate electricity from wastes such as compost, acting as a living battery.

◎ *Decomposers*: When organisms die, they are usually decomposed, or broken down into simple substances, by bacteria and fungi. If this didn't happen, we would be hip-deep in dead dinosaurs and daisies, and there would be no nutrients put back into the environment to make new organisms.

And some of the nasties:

◉ *Yersinia pestis*: This bacteria causes the Bubonic Plague, known as The Black Death in medieval times. It killed more than one third of the population of Europe (about 200 million people) during the 14th century.

Fleas on rats spread the Bubonic Plague during the 14th century.

◉ *Clostridium botulinum*: This bacteria lives in soil, but occasionally makes its way into damaged cans of food. It makes botulinum toxin, which is the most toxic substance of any living thing. It is so toxic, that a teaspoonful (5 ml) in a reservoir supplying water to a major city would be enough to kill everyone in the city who drank it, and 2.2 pounds (1 kg)—the weight of a bag of sugar—could kill every animal in the world. However, if it is greatly diluted, it can be injected into someone's face to make wrinkles less obvious! In this form, it's called Botox.

Fungi

For hundreds of years, people thought of fungi as plants. It made sense: they grew in the ground, they didn't move around, and they didn't seem to eat. But in fact, the organisms in The Fungi Kingdom are very, very different from plants.

The biggest difference is that they can't make their own food. Instead, they make digestive liquids and use them to dissolve dead organisms. This means that, like bacteria, they are important in decomposition. Some of this is useful, but it can also be harmful. **Mildew** can spoil books and clothes, and athlete's foot is a fungus that loves to chomp on damp, dead skin between your toes.

When you think of fungi, you probably think of the mushrooms you can eat, but that's not what all fungi look like. Some fungi are single-celled, such as yeast, which helps bread to rise. It does this when it carries out respiration.

The carbon dioxide yeast produces makes the bread dough rise before baking.

Why is that mushroom dusty?

A mushroom or toadstool is just the reproductive part of a fungus. It doesn't have flowers or seeds. Instead, it produces tiny spores that float away. You can see them if you leave a mushroom cap on a piece of paper for a couple of days. The "dust" left on the paper is actually millions of spores. The rest of the fungus is in the soil, tree trunk, or wherever the fungus is growing. It looks like a net of very thin threads. This is the part of the fungus that digests and takes in food.

Tasty vs deadly

Some fungi are delicious, but others are deadly. Tasty fungi include chanterelles and porcini. Some of the poisonous fungi have wonderful names, such as deathcap, destroying angel, poisonpie, and beechwood sickener. You should never eat wild mushrooms you find outside because they can be very dangerous.

Why did the mushroom get invited to the party? Because he was a fun guy! Get it? He was a fun-gi!

Plantae

A lot of people think plants are boring and that they don't do anything. But they couldn't be more wrong. Life in The Plant Kingdom is just as dramatic and cut-throat as the Animal Kingdom. There are killers, kidnappers, and frauds. It all just happens in slow motion...

Nutrition

Plants contain a green pigment called chlorophyll. This allows them to use the energy in sunlight to make their own food from carbon dioxide and water. They can absorb the other minerals they need through their roots. Almost every other living thing depends on plants' abilities to carry out photosynthesis, either because they eat plants, or they eat animals that eat plants.

However, plants that live in waterlogged soil, such as bogs, can have trouble getting enough of a nutrient called nitrogen. They solve this by becoming killers.

Killers

These killers are the insectivorous plants such as Venus flytraps and pitcher plants. Venus flytraps have special pairs of leaves that have sensitive hairs on them. If an insect touches three of these hairs, the leaf trap closes quickly, and the more the insect struggles, the tighter it closes. Once it has trapped an insect, the leaves produce liquid that digests the insect's body, and the plant absorbs the nutrients.

Pitcher plants attract flies by releasing a smell like dead meat. The inside of the pitcher (a modified leaf) is very slippery and the shape makes it difficult for the flies to get out. If they fall into the pool of digestive liquid at the bottom of the pitcher, they meet their doom.

Growth

Different plants grow at different rates and to different heights. The fastest growing plants are bamboos. Some of them can grow more than 3 feet (1 m) a day!

The largest plant in the world is the Hyperion—a giant sequoia tree in California. It is more than 379 feet (115 m) tall!

One of the slowest growing plants is *Puya raimondii*, which normally lives high in the Bolivian mountains and can take 80–100 years to grow big enough to flower. Another is the Saguaro cactus (which you often see in Western films). It can live for 200 years, but might only be 1.2 inches (3 cm) tall after the first ten years, and grows only 0.8 to 1.2 inches (2–3 cm) per year.

Plant reproduction

Many, but not all, plants reproduce by using flowers to make male pollen and female **ovules**. These have to be transferred from one flower to another for fertilization to take place and seeds to be formed. Some flowering plants only rely on the wind to blow their pollen to another flower, while others rely on insects, birds, bats, mice, and even lizards to carry the pollen from one flower to another. Some plants use bribery to attract creatures, making sweet, sugary nectar for them to drink. Other plants play tricks…

Kidnappers

The giant water lily gives off a pineapple-like scent and only opens in the evening. When a beetle crawls in, the flower shuts around it, trapping it inside for the night. When the flower opens the next evening, the beetle flies away covered in pollen. It carries the pollen to another lily flower, which fertilizes the ovules. The lily that trapped the beetle closes up and sinks into the water, where more seeds develop.

Frauds

Hammer orchids are the frauds of the plant world. They have flowers that look and smell like the flightless females of a species of wasp. The male wasp comes along looking for love, and he tries to carry off a mate. But instead, another part of the flower hits him on the head, covering him in pollen. The male wasp then flies to the next flower that has a pretend female wasp. When he gets hit again, the pollen he is carrying gets transferred to the second flower.

What does he get out of this? Nothing (except possibly a headache).

Sensitivity

Plants are most sensitive to light, and will change their direction of growth so that their leaves get as much light as possible. You see this happen if you keep a plant by a window. It bends toward the light. They are also sensitive to gravity, which is why roots always grow down and shoots always grow up. If they couldn't do this, you would have to make sure every seed you planted was the right way up! Some plants, such as the Venus flytrap and the *mimosa pudica*, or "sensitive plant," are sensitive to touch. Plants such as bindweed, peas, and beans, will twine around anything they touch. This allows them to grow higher without needing a strong stem of their own.

Animalia

The Animal Kingdom covers everything from sponges to humans. There are a lot of different types of organisms in The Animal Kingdom. To avoid any confusion, let's break them down further and look at each of the main phyla one by one. The phyla are the second step of classifying organisms, following Kingdoms.

Phylum Cnidaria

Cnidarians includes sea jellies, sea anemones, and corals. Most of them live in the sea. They have very simple bodies—no head, arms, legs, brain, or heart—but they do have tentacles with stinging cells which they use to catch their food. Sea jellies range from the peanut-sized and deadly **venomous** Irukandji to the huge lion's mane, which can be the size of a small car!

Corals are tiny animals that live in huge colonies. Many have a stony external skeleton, and these build up over many years to form coral reefs such as the Great Barrier Reef.

Phylum Platyhelminthes

Flatworms are simple, soft-bodied worms, with one opening that serves as a mouth and an **anus**. This group includes a lot of worms you don't want to meet, such as tapeworms, blood flukes, and New Zealand flatworms.

Tapeworms live in the guts of mammals. In humans, they can grow to 33 feet (10 m) long. People get them by eating undercooked meat that contains tapeworm eggs. But not all flatworms are harmful. If you have a pond, look carefully at the bottom. You might see tiny harmless flatworms that are 0.2 to 0.4 inches (5–10 mm) long, gliding around. These are called planarians. When you look at them through a magnifying glass, you can see tiny spots at the front end. These are very simple eyes, which can tell light from dark, but not much else.

Phylum Echinodermata

Echinoderms are the group that includes sea stars, sea urchins, and sea cucumbers. They have a separate mouth and anus, but no head or circulatory system.

They all live in the sea and have what's called radial symmetry, which means they are shaped a bit like a pie that you could cut into identical pieces.

Most sea stars have five arms, with a lot of tube feet on each arm so they can creep around the seabed to eat. If one of their arms gets damaged, they can grow a new one, as long as part of the center disk remains!

Sea urchins and sea cucumbers

Sea urchins and sea cucumbers don't look as though they are closely related to sea stars, but they are. If a sea star's arms were all pulled together above its middle, it would be pumpkin-shaped like a sea urchin. If it stretched out as long as possible, it would be shaped like a sea cucumber.

Sea cucumbers have a strange way of defending themselves if something tries to eat them. They throw up the food in their stomach, along with their whole stomach as well! This sticks all over whatever is attacking them, giving them time to creep away, but leaving them with a problem. How do you eat when your stomach is gone? Here's the really amazing part—they grow a new one!

Phylum Nematoda

Roundworms are—you guessed it—round. Roundworms are more complicated than flatworms because they have a nervous system, but they have no circulatory system.

Some roundworms are **parasites** that live in the digestive tracts of animals such as cats, dogs, humans, and whales. (Roundworms in whales can be several feet long.) Roundworms, sometimes called nematodes, can also be pests in plants, and live in soil in huge numbers. There may be hundreds in 2.2 pounds (1 kg) of soil. But they are so small, you need a microscope to see most of them.

A giant Australian worm can live up to 20 years!

Phylum Annelida

Scientists file earthworms, leeches, and other segmented worms in the Annelids group. Segments are repeated units—like the segments of an orange. Each segment of a worm has the same basic structures inside. They have a proper digestive tract, a nervous system, and a circulatory system.

Earthworm

Leeches

Leeches live in water or in very damp places. Some are predators, but many are parasites, which feed by sucking blood from other animals. There are many leech species that feed on fish blood, but some target birds or mammals—including humans. They can survive for a year on a single blood meal. When a leech bites, it injects a local anaesthetic which freezes the area, so the animal doesn't feel the bite. It also injects an **anticoagulant** chemical to stop the blood from clotting. Crafty!

Leech

Earthworms

Did you know that soil is basically earthworm droppings? The worms eat dead and decaying leaves, and when they get rid of their waste, it forms soil. The holes they dig help with drainage. So if you want good soil, you need earthworms. The biggest earthworms are found in Australia, and can be more than 10 feet (3 m) long!

Leech medicine

For hundreds of years, leeches were used in medicine because doctors thought a lot of diseases could be cured by slowly draining people's blood. They were wrong, of course, and the practice died out. However, leeches are being used in modern surgery. They're the best way to keep blood flowing through a reattached finger after surgery. New anticoagulant drugs based on leeches have also been developed.

Small garden snail.

Phylum Mollusca

Mollusks have soft, squashy bodies, and many of them have a shell which protects them. They have a heart, a circulatory system, and a complex nervous system. Most, but not all, live in water. They include snails, slugs, mussels, oysters, octopuses, and squid.

Snails and slugs are very similar. A big difference is that snails have shells they can retreat into, whereas slugs don't. They both have rough tongues that feel like a nail file, and eat by scraping away at plant leaves. The giant African land snail is the largest, and can weigh up to 2.2 pounds (1 kg).

giant African land snail

Snails

Snails are **hermaphrodites**, which means each snail is male and female at the same time. You might think this means a snail can reproduce on its own, but it still needs a partner.

To decide who is going to do what, the snails shoot "love darts" at each other. These are tiny spikes which mating snails try to stab into each other. The one who stabs first is more likely to end up as the male in the mating process. And you thought snails were boring!

Some gardeners put copper strips around plant pots to keep snails away. It works because the copper gives snails an electric shock!

Bivalves

A bivalve is a mollusk with a pair of shells. There are over 10,000 species, including cockles, mussels, and oysters. Some live in fresh water, but most are found in the sea. When they are underwater, their shells are open. Water flows through the bivalve, and they filter out tiny bits of food. If oysters or mussels get a bit of grit, or sans, stuck in them, they produce a substance called nacre and wrap the grit in it to protect themselves from irritation. Layers of nacre eventually build up to form a pearl.

Unlike snails and slugs, bivalves don't have a head and adults don't move around. To reproduce, they release a lot of **gametes** into the sea, and it's just a matter of luck if two of the same species meet up. If they do, they produce a tiny larva. That larva swims around until it finds the right kind of rock, where it settles down for the rest of its life.

Ming the clam was probably the oldest animal in the world, until scientists accidentally killed him. He lived on the seabed near Iceland, and was accidentally frozen to death with 199 other clams. The clams were were being taken to a laboratory to be studied. When counting the clams' age rings, the scientists discovered Ming. They found out he was 507 years old before he died.

Octopus, squid, and cuttlefish

Octopuses have eight arms, and squid and cuttlefish have ten. If they are threatened, they shoot a cloud of black ink into the water to confuse their predators. They then escape by jet-propelling themselves with a blast of water. Their skin can also change color and pattern very quickly. They use this to communicate and to camouflage themselves. Mimic octopuses also have the ability to change their body shape, giving them the appearance of a completely different animal! Octopuses can also use tools. They can unscrew a lid to get at prey, hide under shells, and solve mazes.

Phylum Arthropoda

Arthropods are the largest and most important invertebrate phylum, so we'll look at it class by class. (Remember, each phylum is divided into classes.) The four classes of Arthropods are Insects, Arachnids, Myriapods, and Crustaceans.

Class Insecta

Insects have six legs, and bodies divided into three parts: head, thorax, and abdomen. Many, but not all, insects, have two pairs of wings. Insects are the most successful and widespread animal group on Earth, with at least one million species.

From the largest... to the smallest...

The largest insect is probably the Goliath beetle, which weighs 4 ounces (115 g) and can grow to be 4.5 inches (11.5 cm) long. The longest insects are stick insects, with the record being 22 inches (56.7 cm).

The largest butterfly in the world is the Queen Alexandra's birdwing, with a wingspan of 11 inches (28 cm). But there are some very small insects, too.

11 in. (28cm) wingspan

The smallest insects are fairyflies, which are actually tiny wasps. They can be as small as 0.006 inches (0.14 mm) in length. That's smaller than some single-celled organisms. Yet, they have digestive, reproductive, circulatory, and nervous systems packed in there.

Small, but deadly...

Some insects can be extremely dangerous. Mosquitoes kill millions of people by transmitting malaria. Fleas transmitted the bacteria of the Bubonic Plague. Tsetse flies spread sleeping sickness, which kills hundreds of thousands of people in Africa every year.

Long distance travelers

Insects can travel great distances. The Monarch butterfly flies about 4,350 miles (7,000 km) in an annual **migration** from Mexico to Southern Canada and back. However, it takes four generations of butterflies to do this.

The globe skimmer dragonfly beat that distance by a long way. It appears to migrate from southern India to southern Africa, and back again— that's 8,700 miles (14,000 km). It also takes four generations to finish the trip.

Did you know there are over 350,000 different species of beetles in the world?

Class Arachnida

Arachnids have four pairs of legs and include spiders, mites, and scorpions.

Spiders

House spiders are harmless and helpful, eating all sorts of potentially annoying insects. However, spiders in certain countries can be quite hazardous. The bites of the black widow and redback spiders can be fatal.

Spider silk is produced by organs called spinnerets at the back of the abdomen. The silk is used by spiders to make webs, nets, nests, and cocoons. It is a very light and thin substance, but is extremely strong. Researchers are extremely interested in the silk, and have **genetically modified** bacteria, plants, and even goats to be able to produce it! Some researchers used over one million Golden Orb spiders to create a cape made of spider silk. It look three years to produce.

Mites

You may not have seen a mite before, but if you have a pet dog or cat that scratches its ears a lot, it may have mites in them. If you have asthma, it may be triggered by the droppings of house dust mites.

Some mites have very strange life cycles. The strangest of all is the mite *Acarophenax tribolii*. Fifteen eggs develop and hatch inside the female mite. One is male and the others are all female. The male mates with all his sisters and promptly dies. The females, each now containing 15 developing eggs, eat their way out of their mother—while she's still alive—and the whole cycle begins again!

Scorpions

Scorpions have a very distinctive body shape. They have large front claws, four pairs of walking legs, and a curving, **venomous** stinger. But did you know they also glow in the dark? Their cuticle, or outer covering, is fluorescent under UV light, although it looks black in daylight.

Out of around 1,000 species of scorpions, only 25 have venom that is deadly to humans. Although many of the others can cause you a lot of pain. Generally, scorpions with big claws and small stingers aren't very venomous. But if they have small claws and a big stinger, they are. Scorpion venoms are now being investigated for medical use.

Scorpion under UV light.

Class Myriapoda

There are two types of Myriapods— centipedes and millipedes. These are animals with many body segments and even more legs. How many legs does a myriapod have? It depends… The fewest has ten, and the most has around 750!

Don't worry, this millipede is about three times bigger than the real ones!

Millipedes

Millipedes have two pairs of legs on each body segment. They don't tend to be as fast moving as centipedes. However, they don't have to be because they eat plants, not other animals. The largest known millipede measured more than 14.6 inches (37 cm).

Centipedes

Centipedes are fast on their numerous feet. They have to be, since they are predators—many have a venomous bite. The biggest centipedes can be more than 12 inches (30 cm) long. They have one pair of legs on each of their body segments.

Class Crustacea

Shrimps, prawns, lobsters, crabs, and woodlice are all crustaceans. Woodlice are the odd ones out in this group because they are the only members that live on land. You can find them in your garden, under flower pots, or in pieces of rotting wood. All the others live in the sea or fresh water.

Woodlice are crustaceans which live on land.

Barnacles

Barnacles spend all of their adult life in a shell, stuck to a rock. They actually stand on their heads, kicking food into their mouths. They are the white, crusty things found on rocks at the seaside, but they will also grow on the underside of boats, and even on the skin of whales! This doesn't harm the whale—its skin is so thick that it doesn't even notice. Some crustaceans, however, are parasites.

Barnacles might be one of the oldest surviving creatures on the planet. It's believed that they haven't changed very much over that time.

Nasty parasites

The nastiest crustacean is the tongue-eating louse. This horrible parasite gets into a fish through its gills. It then attaches itself to the fish's tongue and extracts the blood from it with its claws. Then it takes the place of the tongue once it has been destroyed.

barnacles

whale

How big?

Crustaceans come in many different sizes. Horseshoe crabs can be up to 2 feet (60 cm) long, and the giant amphipod—a deep sea version of a woodlouse—can be 18 inches (45 cm) long! Imagine if that was in your back garden, not deep in the sea!

The smallest crustacean is *Stygotantulus stocki*. It is less than 0.004 inches (0.1 mm) long, and lives as a parasite on other small crustaceans.

Mantis shrimp

Horseshoe crab

Super shrimp

One of the most impressive crustaceans is the mantis shrimp. Mantis shrimp have the most complex eyes of any animal. They can see in the UV and infrared parts of the **spectrum**, as well as in normal light. Their front legs are adapted into spears or clubs, depending on the species. They can whack their prey with enough force to shatter the glass of an aquarium tank.

Phylum Chordata

The final phylum is Chordata, sometimes called the Vertebrates, which contains most of the animals we come across or hear about in our day-to-day life—including us! Their defining characteristics are that they have a spinal cord and a tail at some point in their lives. Most of them also have a backbone and a bony skeleton. This is another huge group, so we'll look at it class by class.

Class Fish

This class is made up of many different classes of fish. To qualify as a fish, you need to live in water, swim using muscles and fins, be covered in scales, breathe using gills, and lay eggs in water.

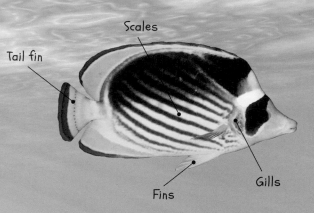

Tail fin

Scales

Fins

Gills

Sharks

Sharks are fish, but their skeletons are made of **cartilage** (like the squishy stuff at the end of your nose), and they have rough skin instead of scales. There are more than 400 species of shark. They range from the small zebra shark, which is gentle enough to share an aquarium with other fish, to the great white, which will attack almost anything—including people. There is also a wide variety of weird-looking sharks, including the whale shark, which is the world's largest fish; the basking shark, which has one of the world's largest mouths; and the deeply strange goblin shark and hammerhead shark.

Goblin shark

Hammerhead shark

Amazing eels

In estuaries all over Europe, thousands of tiny transparent glass eels head up river from the sea. Once they get into fresh water, they develop into elvers (small versions of adult eels) and start feeding. They spend 5 to 20 years in the rivers, developing to yellow eels, then to silver eels. They then head back out to sea to breed. They swim more than 3,728 miles (6,000 km) to the Sargasso Sea off the west coast of America to lay their eggs in the water. These eggs hatch into tiny larvae, which swim all the way back again—a journey that can take another three years! They change into glass eels and the whole cycle starts again.

Fresh or salt?

A goldfish is a good example of a fish that lives in fresh water. It might be a surprise to learn that these freshwater fish don't drink the water. This is because they take in water all over their body surface. They lose all this water by urinating, or peeing, often.

Fish that live in the sea actually lose water all the time, so they do drink water, and pee as little as possible. Haddock and cod—which you have probably eaten if you like fish and chips—are good examples of sea fish.

Some fish, such as salmon and eels, live part of their lives in fresh water and part in the sea. They have to undergo a sort of Clark Kent-to-Superman change when they move from one type of water to the other.

Doting dads

Seahorses don't look like fish, but they actually are, and they have a very unusual way of reproducing. It all starts when the male and female spend hours dancing together as part of their courtship. When they're convinced they've found the perfect partner, the female lays her eggs into a pouch a bit like a tiny kangaroo's pouch on the male's tummy. The eggs get fertilized here, so it's the male who gets pregnant. He may have 2,000 babies! Once he gives birth though, he's done his job, and the babies have to fend for themselves.

Pygmy seahorses are tiny and well camouflaged. They are difficult to spot among soft corals. Can you spot one?

Pygmy seahorse

Class Amphibia

Amphibians include frogs, toads, and newts. They have moist, naked skin through which they can absorb oxygen, and lungs when they are adults. They spend time on land and in water, where they lay eggs. Young amphibians, called tadpoles, live in water, breathe through gills, and look like fish before they undergo a huge change called **metamorphosis**. This is a process through which they develop their final body shape.

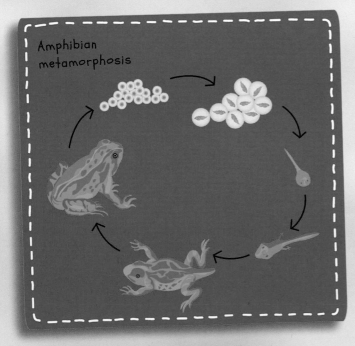

Amphibian metamorphosis

Spectacular superhero skills

Don't underestimate amphibians! They have a range of powers that would make any superhero envious! Read on to discover some spectacular superhero skills that amphibians possess.

Frogs and toads catch insects by flicking their sticky tongues out at high speed to hit them. Their tongues are attached at the front, not at the back like ours, so they can shoot out very fast.

🐸 Frogs close their eyes when they swallow, not because they're savoring the taste of a delicious fly, but because they use pressure from their eyeballs to help push the food into their throats.

Wood frog in snow

🐸 North American wood frogs can freeze solid in very cold winter weather. Their hearts stop and they can be encased in ice—in other words, they're dead. They can stay like this for weeks, but when they thaw out, they come back to life! They use this incredible ability to survive temperatures as low as 0°F (–18°C).

🐸 Iberian ribbed newts push their own ribs through their skin to make temporary spines if they are attacked. Since they also have toxic skin, this discourages a lot of predators from eating them.

🐸 A 2-inch (5 cm) long golden poison dart frog has enough poison on its skin to kill 10–20 people. It may be the most poisonous animal on Earth.

Golden Poison dart frog

Class Reptilia

Reptiles have dry skin which is covered in scales. They lay leathery-shelled eggs on land. Some live on land and others live in water. They include lizards, snakes, turtles, tortoises, and crocodiles.

Tortoises and turtles

Tortoises and turtles can live for a very long time. The oldest recorded tortoise was Tu'i Malila, who was reputedly given to the King of Tonga by Captain Cook in 1777. The tortoise was 189 when it died in 1965.

In most animals, the gender of a baby depends on the type of sex chromosomes it has. But in many reptiles, it depends on the temperature at which the eggs develop. Turtle eggs develop into males in cool conditions, and into females in warm conditions.

Komodo dragon

Lizards

The biggest and most fearsome lizard in the world is the Komodo dragon. It can grow to be 10 feet (3 m) long and weigh up to 165 pounds (75 kg). They are fast and ferocious predators. They can attack humans, as well as other large animals (including other Komodo dragons), although they will also eat dead animals.

Many chameleons can change their skin color to blend into the background. They have eyes that can move independently, so they can look in two directions at once, and a long tongue that can shoot out at high speed. These adaptations make them very good hunters.

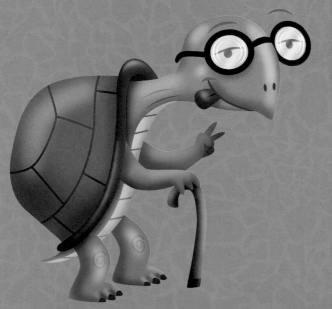

Snakes

Snakes have two main methods of hunting. Constrictors crush their prey by wrapping themselves around the animal and squeezing. Some constrictors are huge. Anacondas can be more than 23 feet (7 m) long, and can go for a year without eating. (They would need to eat something pretty big first, though—the snake equivalent of Christmas dinner).

Boa constrictor

Venomous snakes kill with a bite. The most venomous snake of all is the Inland Taipan. Some snakes have special areas on their face that allow them to detect **infrared** radiation from other living things. This means that they can catch and kill prey in total darkness.

Crocodiles and alligators

What's the difference? Alligators are only found in the United States and China, whereas crocodiles live in Africa, Asia, Australia, and the Americas. An alligator's snout is long, narrow, and pointy, whereas a crocodile's snout is shorter, wider, and rounder. Alligators are generally only found in fresh water, whereas some crocodiles live in salt water.

Like turtles, the gender of crocodiles and alligators depend on the temperature at which the eggs develop. They will all be females at low or high temperatures, and males at medium temperatures.

Class Aves

Birds have bodies covered in feathers. They have wings instead of front legs, and beaks instead of teeth. They can also keep their body temperature stable, independent from the temperature of their surroundings. They breathe using lungs and lay hard-shelled eggs to reproduce.

Fabulous bird facts

Birds range in size from the tiny bee hummingbird, with a mass of 0.06 to 0.07 ounces (1.6–1.9 g); to the huge ostrich, which weighs in at more than 220 pounds (100 kg). The ostrich can't fly, and has very small wings for its size. The largest wingspan belongs to the wandering albatross, at 11.5 feet (3.5 m). The cassowary is nearly as big as an ostrich, and is probably the most dangerous bird in the world—one kick of its mighty legs can seriously injure someone.

Cassowary

Speedy!

Some birds can move very fast! A peregrine falcon can reach nearly 250 miles per hour (400 kph) in a hunting dive, and an ostrich can reach up to 56 miles per hour (90 kph) when it's running. The fastest swimmers are gentoo penguins, which can whizz along underwater at 25 miles per hour (40 kph).

Grey owl

Cave swiftlets use saliva to glue their nests to the rocks inside caves!

Serious senses

Birds have amazing senses. Some species of owls have feathers on their faces that focus sound similar to a satellite dish receiver. The great grey owl has such good hearing that it can hunt mice moving under snowdrifts.

Cave swiftlets and oilbirds can avoid obstacles in total darkness by using **echolocation**, which is a way of detecting objects by bouncing sound waves off them.

Many birds, such as pigeons, can detect Earth's magnetic field and use it to **navigate**. This is how homing pigeons are able to find their way back home.

Class: Mammalia

Mammals make up the group to which humans belong. Mammals have hairy or furry skin, breathe using lungs, and can control their body temperature like birds. The young of most mammals develop inside the uterus of the mother's body, and are fed on her milk once they are born. These are called placental mammals.

Monotremes

These are mammals that lay eggs instead of giving birth to live young. There are five species—four types of echidnas (or spiny anteaters), and the duck-billed platypus. When scientists first saw a platypus, they thought it must be a hoax! Who would have believed there was an egg-laying mammal with a duck's bill, a tail like a beaver, and venomous spurs on its legs?

Marsupials

Marsupials, such as kangaroos and wombats, don't lay eggs, but their young don't develop for very long inside the mother's body. Instead, they are born very poorly developed and very tiny. A newborn kangaroo only weighs about 0.07 ounces (2 g)—about the same as a jelly bean. They have to crawl over the mother's fur to a special pouch where they will stay and grow for several months. All the mammals that are native to Australia are either egg-layers or marsupials, but placental mammals were introduced by ship when humans arrived. These mammals were more successful at reproducing, causing many native marsupial species to die out.

> Most mammals have four legs which they use to walk or run, and live on land. But of course, there are some exceptions.

Bats

Bats have a web of skin between their front and hind legs that they use as wings. They are excellent fliers, but useless at moving around on the ground. They fly at night, and rely on echolocation to steer and hunt.

Whales, porpoises, and dolphins, oh my!

Whales, porpoises, and dolphins are mammals—not fish! They have flippers and a tail instead of limbs. Their bodies are very streamlined, which allows them to move quickly through water. The blue whale is the largest animal that ever lived—it can grow to be 98 feet (30 m) long and weigh 220 tons (200 metric tons). Their tongues weigh as much as a fully grown elephant!

The blue whale gets to this size on a diet mostly made up of tiny shrimp-like animals called krill, but they eat up to 4.4 tons (4 metric tons) of them a day. They don't crunch them up with teeth, because they don't have any. Instead they have a huge filter in their mouths made of a material called **baleen**.

> How did I get here?

> Uh...oh... ???

Class: Primates

Mammals include humans, and our closest relatives among them are the Great Apes: orangutans, gorillas, chimpanzees, and bonobos. None of them have tails, even though that is a defining characteristic of a mammal. They do have tails as embryos though, when they are developing into babies in their mother's bodies. But they reabsorb them long before they are born, just like a tadpole does when it turns into a frog.

Locations of the Great Apes throughout the world

All Great Apes live in Africa, except the orangutan, which lives in Sumatra and Borneo. They are all endangered species, due to habitat loss, hunting, and the effects of **civil war**. They can all use tools, but chimpanzees and bonobos use them best. Some apes have been taught to communicate with people using sign language.

The chimpanzee was the first non-human animal that was recorded using tools.

Bonobos

Our closest relatives of all are the bonobos, which used to be called pygmy chimpanzees. We share about 98% of our genetic makeup with them—while tigers and domestic cats only share 96% of their genes with each other.

Kanzi, a 35-year-old bonobo, can communicate using 348 special symbols on a keyboard, and he understands many spoken words. He lives with members of his family in an ape sanctuary with plenty of outdoor space. Their house includes a kitchen with a microwave and vending machine which they can operate, and a computer on which they watch DVDs of their choice. If Kanzi is given marshmallows and matches, he can build a fire and toast marshmallows on a twig.

He may be the smartest non-human on Earth!

Bonobos are our distant cousins and they are very smart.

Class Hominidae

We'll end our tour of life on Earth by looking at our own species—*Homo sapiens*. It's easy to think of humans as something special, but are we really any more special than an orchid that pretends to be a wasp, a frog that can survive freezing temperatures, or a bonobo that can toast marshmallows on a fire he built by himself? And if we are different, what makes us different?

Appearance

Well, we certainly look a bit different from the Great Apes. We are much less hairy, so we wear clothes to stay warm, and we are far more upright when we stand and walk. We aren't as strong as chimpanzees, but our control over our muscles is much more exact, so our movements can be more precise. Our jaws, lips, tongues, and the vocal cords in our throats are different from those of the apes as well, which means we can make a far larger range of sounds. Humans, unlike apes, can communicate very complicated ideas in a spoken language.

Brilliant brains

It's our brains that really set us apart from our nearest relatives. They are much larger in comparison to our body size than ape brains, and they have many more connections between the various parts. We can think in ways that simply aren't possible for any other species. This allows us to use symbols to communicate, which is what is happening now as you read the patterns of ink on paper that form this book. It also lets us think of new ideas, from something as simple as the design of a paperclip, to theories about how life on Earth began…

Wonderful life

Life on Earth is a huge subject to tackle in a book like this. For every organism included here, there are tens of thousands that couldn't fit in. The most amazing thing is that every one of them is unique and wonderful in its own way. Every bacterium, fungus, cactus, wasp, and shark—and every other living thing—is fantastically well suited to its own particular way of life. A snail is just as fascinating and beautiful as a tiger, if you look at it properly.

Looking after life

We are the only species that can study other organisms. We are the only species that can try to understand how all the other organisms work, and what they need to survive. And we are certainly the only species capable of appreciating how precious all the other species are.

It's our responsibility to try to look after life on Earth. Not just the cute and cuddly parts, but life in all its scaly, slimy, prickly, squishy glory!

Try It Yourself

Which way is up?

Gardening would take much longer if you had to plant every seed the right way up. We don't usually see what happens to upside-down seeds, because they are underground, but you can find out by doing a simple experiment.

You will need:

- Broad bean seeds
- Sewing pins
- A piece of florist's foam
- An empty plastic tub, big enough to hold the foam and leave a bit of space around the sides

What to do:

1. Soak a few beans in water overnight. Soak the florist's foam at the same time.
2. The next day, use the sewing pins to attach the beans to the sides of the florist's foam. Some beans should be the right way up, some sideways, and some upside down.
3. Put the florist's foam in the tub. Add water so it is standing in a shallow pool of water, but the water doesn't reach the beans (or they will rot).
4. Look at the beans every day. Watch the roots and shoots change the direction they grow until the roots head down and the shoots head up. Remember to keep the foam wet!
5. When you finish the experiment, you can plant the beans in a pot of soil or in the garden.

What do woodlice want?

If you look under pots or logs in your garden or schoolyard, you might find some woodlice. If you collect some, you can carry out an investigation into what conditions they prefer. Don't worry about picking them up—they are completely harmless.

What you need:
- 10–20 woodlice
- An empty shoebox or big plastic tub
- Some black paper or fabric
- Gravel, dead leaves, sand, soil, small stones— you may be able to think of other things, too.

What to do:
1. Investigate whether your woodlice prefer light or dark. Put them in the shoebox, but don't put the lid on, and let them get used to it for 5–10 minutes.

2. Now, cover half the box with the black paper or cloth. Leave the experiment for 20 minutes, then see where the woodlice are. Most of them will probably prefer darkness.

3. Make different areas in your shoebox using the gravel and other substances you have collected. Try to make some damp areas and some dry areas.

4. Release your woodlice into their hotel and put the lid on the box. Leave them overnight, then count how many have chosen each area. Woodlice usually prefer dark and damp conditions, and like to be under cover. This makes sense because it keeps them hidden from animals that would like to eat them, and prevents them from drying out.

Wildlife expert

You can become a wildlife expert without having to go somewhere exotic!

- If you have a garden, spend some time really getting to know the wildlife there. If not, you could try a nearby field, park, or your schoolyard.

- Put out bird food and learn to identify the birds that visit your garden. This site will help you figure out what bird you're watching: http://animals.nationalgeographic.com/animals/birding/backyard-bird-identifier/

- Watch for butterflies and get involved in the next Big Butterfly Count: www.naba.org/pubs/countpub.html

Find Out More

This book only has space for a very brief introduction to this enormous and wonderful subject. If it has sparked your interest in any sort of living thing, you can easily find out lots more about it.

Visit

Take a trip to a zoo, wildlife park, butterfly farm, bird of prey center, urban farm, botanical garden, or nature reserve. If you can't get to any of these, have a look at webcam feeds from zoos all over the world at www.thezooonline.com/

Read

"A Class of Their Own" Series. Crabtree Publishing, 2010.

Durrell, Gerald. *My Family and Other Animals. 3rd ed.* Penguin Books: 2004.

Watch

Anything narrated or presented by David Attenborough. He gets excited about anything from a blue whale to a head louse, and makes you understand how wonderful each of them is!

You can see Kanzi the Bonobo building a fire and toasting marshmallows at www.youtube.com/watch?v=GQcN7lHSD5Y

Log on to

Explore the world of bugs and other creepy crawlies at: http://pestworldforkids.org

This interactive website is full of information on many types of animals: www.skyenimals.com/

Glossary

AIDS A disease of the immune system that makes it difficult for the body to fight off infections

Amino acids "Building blocks" used in every cell of the body to build proteins

Anticoagulant Substance that stops blood clotting

Anus An opening at the end of an animal's body through which solid waste is excreted

Asexual reproduction Organisms producing offspring (new organisms) on their own, without the need for both male and female cells

Asteroids Small rocky objects in space that orbit the Sun

Bacteria Simple single-celled organisms that are found all over the world, including in the human body

Bacteriophage Virus that infects and reproduces inside bacteria

Baleen Strong material in a whale's mouth that is made out of keratin (the protein that our hair and fingernails are made from)

Cartilage Slippery material that covers the ends of bones and joints, and forms ears and noses of people

Chlorophyll Green pigment found in plants

Civil war War between groups of people from the same country or state

Classification Putting things into classes or categories

DNA Material in an organism that carries all the information about how it will look and work

Echolocation Making sounds and using the echoes from the sounds to figure out where objects are

Eukaryotic cells Cells that contain a nucleus and other parts

Excretion Getting rid of waste products that have been made by an organism

Gamete Cell that fuses with another cell during fertilization to form a new organism

Genetically modified When organisms have had their DNA changed in a non-natural way

Hermaphrodite Organism with both male and female reproductive organs

Homo sapiens Scientific name for the human species

Infrared Invisible electromagnetic radiation with a wavelength longer than visible light

Irreversible Not possible to change back

Latin A language originally spoken in ancient Rome, but now used for scientific names of organisms

61

Locomotion Movement from place to place

Malaria Often fatal disease carried by mosquitoes, causing a high fever and chills

Metamorphosis Complete change in body form (from young to adult)

Meteorite Rock that falls to Earth from space

Migration Movement of animals from one region to another

Mildew Thin fungus growth

Molecules Groups of atoms (body "building blocks") bonded together

Multicellular Made up of many different cells

Navigate Find your way around

Nucleus Part of a cell that controls what happens in the cell

Nutrition Getting the food needed for growth and health

Offspring New organisms

Ovule The female reproductive cells of plants

Parasite Organism living in or on another organism, often causing harm to the other organism

Photosynthesis Process used by plants to convert carbon dioxide and water into food, using energy from sunlight

Primordial Very first, earliest

Prokaryotic cells Simple cells that do not contain a nucleus and are only found in bacteria

Proteins Essential part of all living organisms (part of the muscle, skin, and bones in humans)

Radiation Energy in the form of electromagnetic waves

Respiration Breaking down food in cells to release energy

Sexual reproduction Organisms producing offspring (new organisms) using both male and female cells that join together

Smallpox Often fatal disease. Those infected have a fever and blisters all over the skin

Spectrum Band or scale

Spore Small single-celled body that can grow into a new organism

Toxic Poisonous

Ultraviolet radiation (UV) Invisible electromagnetic radiation from the Sun with a wavelength shorter than visible light

Venomous Poisonous

Virus Organism that infects cells and reproduces inside them

Index

age of Earth 6
alligators 49
amino acids 6
amphibians 46–47
anacondas 49
animal cell structure 13
annelids 32–33
arachnids 38–39
arthropods 36–39
asexual reproduction 9
athlete's foot 24
atmosphere 6

bacteria 9, 12, 13, 16, 20, 21, 22–23, 36, 38
bacteriophages 20
bamboos 27
barnacles 40
bats 53
bee hummingbirds 50
beginning of life on Earth 6–7
birds 50–51
bivalves 35
bonobos 54, 55, 60
Botox 23
botulinum toxin 23
brains 9, 13, 15, 30, 56
Bubonic Plague 23, 36
butterflies 36–37

carbon dioxide 6, 11, 24, 26
cassowaries 50
cave swiftlets 51
cell, definition of 12
cell membrane 12, 13
cell structure 12–13
cell wall 13
cells 8, 9, 10, 11, 12–15, 20, 21, 22, 24, 30
centipedes 39
changes in environment 9
chlorophyll 11, 26
chloroplasts 13
chordates 42–45
clams 36

classification of organisms 16–17
cnidarians 30
comet 7
communication 56
constrictors 49
corals 30
crocodiles 49
crustaceans 40–41
cuttlefish 35
cytoplasm 12, 13

decomposition 22, 24
diseases 20, 21, 23, 36
DNA 6, 12, 20
dolphins 53
duck-billed platypus 52

earthworms 32–33
echinoderms 31
eels 44
endangered species 54
energy 6, 10, 26
eukaryotic cells 12
excretion 11

fertilization 28
fish 43–44
flatworms 31, 32
fleas 36
foxglove names 18–19
fresh water 44
frogs 46–47
fungi 12, 16, 21, 24–25

gardening 58
genus 17, 19
gentoo penguins 51
giant water lilies 28
Goliath beetles 36
Great Apes 54–55, 56
growth 9, 10, 27

hammer orchids 29
hermaphrodites 34

Homo sapiens 17, 19, 56–57
Hooke, Robert 12
horseshoe crabs 41
humans 10, 11, 12, 14, 17, 19, 22, 30, 31, 32, 33, 39, 48, 52, 54, 56–57

insects 36

kangaroos 52
Kingdoms 16–17, 20, 21, 22, 24, 26, 30
Komodo dragons 48
krill 53

Latin 18–19
leeches 32–33
life, characteristics of 8–11
life, looking after 57
lightning 6
Linnaeus, Carl 18–19
lizards 48
locomotion 8

malaria 21, 36
mammals 52–53
mantis shrimp 41
marsupials 52
metamorphosis 46
meteorites 7
microscope 12, 21, 32
migration 37
mildew 24
millipedes 39
mites 38
mitochondrion 12, 13
molecules 6–7, 11
mollusks 34–35
monotremes 52
mosquitoes 21, 36
movement 8, 56
multicellular organisms 14, 15
mushrooms 15, 24–25
myriapods 39